CONTENTS

Welcome

"Eat to live and not to die. The Bible teaches us that God, in the end of the world when He comes, will prolong the people's lives because they have been eating the proper foods, both spiritually and physically. We have to accept it—that is, if we love life and not death."

How To Eat To Live - Book Two
by the
The Most Honorable Elijah Muhammad

This cookbook is dedicated to the people of God's Choice who must learn the value of their lives and the importance of eating to live in order for us to preserve the precious gift of Life that the Creator has granted us.

It was Jesus who is quoted in the scriptures as saying that he had come that we would have "...life and have it more abundantly..." This is what we want for you through the recipes found in this book.

These recipes are inspired by the Teachings of the Most Honorable Elijah Muhammad and the Representation of these Teachings by His National Representative, the Honorable Minister Louis Farrakhan.

The principles and structure of the recipes are from the guidance found in How To Eat To Live (Books 1 & 2) by the Most Honorable Elijah Muhammad.

Forward

Producing this cookbook was very humbling to me as a reminder of how truly blessed I am. Clearly, I am blessed with a wonderful wife who can cook. However, the primary blessing isn't just having a spouse with 'crazy' culinary skills. No, the main blessing is to be married to a believing woman in Almighty God and as such, she is desirous, at all times, of doing that which pleases Him.

Therefore, putting together this cookbook was a treat and easy to get motivated for because I know how delicious these dishes really are. When you try a couple of these recipes you will see just how marvelous the dishes are.

For those who are new to shopping for fresh vegetables and fruits, we included some pictures of some of the key ingredients hoping that you will shop for them and not the canned/frozen versions, if possible.

After preparing and tasting these dishes, you will be amazed at how good they taste while being so good for you. But be careful with the power of these meals. You will find it tempting to overeat particularly with the desserts. Just pace yourself so you can truly appreciate this gift from us to you. Your life will be improved by coming back home to Good Dining and Good Health.

Amin Muhammad

THE ORIGINAL MIND

A'ishah's Preface

All throughout my adult life, I have been asked, "where did you learn to cook?" The first reference I always cite is my mother who is an excellent cook. When I was just a little girl, my mother had to work and she also went to school. She would have to leave me instructions on how to prepare certain foods.

I received my first set of cookbooks when I was about six years old, The Women's Day Encyclopedia of Cooking. I still have them; torn, battered and a few books shy of the original set I once had. I had learned the basics of pot roast, baked chicken, steaks and spaghetti sauce before I reached 6th grade. I also spent time with my paternal grandmother who was blind and I watched her carefully measure and prepare pinto beans and other dishes. Nevertheless, all of my old familiar references continue to serve their purpose. Those memories have stayed with me until this day.

Many years later, as a part of the Muslim Girls Training and General Civilization Class (MGT & GCC), my skills were further developed and enhanced. My curiosity about the origins of foods, spices and their combinations kept me reading in search of ideas. As an adult, I was/am always looking for ways to satisfy my tastes and that of my family without sacrificing the flavors and textures I crave.

Ten years ago, I was placed on hypertension medication and after giving birth to my daughter, my blood pressure began to creep up. At some point, I decided that with a family history of both hypertension and diabetes, I had to make some changes in my diet. That decision was sealed when my physician told me that my LDL/HDL (cholesterol levels) were good, but my overall number had to come down.

Even though I already had eliminated meat from my diet 25 years ago, without a second thought, I made the decision to replace certain fatty foods such as 2% milk, butter, cheese and whole eggs with skim milk, non-fat yogurt, olive oil, low-fat or rice cheese, and egg whites. I added flax seed meal to my oatmeal and to my yogurt. I also began to eat lots and lots of garlic. I ate garlic minced, raw in salads, roasted in olive oil and sautéed in vegetables. As a result, I lost weight, my bad cholesterol was reduced and my good cholesterol was elevated. My triglycerides were reduced and I was taken off of hypertension medications. Whenever anyone asks me what "diet" I used, I simply tell them I began to practice eating to live.

So, as a person who loves good food along with good company and after numerous requests, I decided (with the encouragement of my husband) to share these recipes with you. These recipes will delight your palate and hopefully, improve your health.

I asked my sister and friend, Kimberly D. Muhammad, one of the most outstanding cooks and bakers I know, to add her prized recipes to this effort. Our families always socialize over food and have dinner parties from time to time. At these affairs, those who are unfamiliar with our culinary skills express disbelief over what they thought were old familiar favorite dishes, but what was in fact tastier and healthier alternatives to what they were used to eating.

We have learned to replace sweet potatoes with carrot souffle; yams are replaced with butternut squash, and corn bread is replaced by farina muffins. We have learned that both sweet potatoes and corn meal are very taxing on the stomach and not the best foods for your overall health. In other words, we love our lives and we love to eat therefore, our recipes help us to eat to live.

Kim always says, "They'd better ask somebody; they don't know. There's nothing like eating good food that is healthy." We don't need to deprive ourselves in our effort to improve our health or lose weight, we just need to make better choices in what we eat and practice moderation.

These recipes are intended to help you improve both your diet and your dining experience. Of course, all of this will be easy to do once you taste the savory dishes given to you in this book.

Had it not been for the Honorable Minister Louis Farrakhan, I would not have been encouraged or inspired to do this, nor would I have had the opportunity to share with so many what Allah has given me.

Please learn to appreciate the value of your life; the most precious thing you possess. You can enjoy delicious food, savory dishes and delightful desserts while respecting, treasuring and enjoying your life. Read How To Eat To Live by the Most Honorable Elijah Muhammad and refer to it often and hopefully you will be inspired as countless others have been to add to the quality of your life.

Peace and love,

A'ishah

KIM'S PREFACE

I would like to thank God for my mother and grandmother who laid for me the foundation for the art and joy of cooking. While growing up, I can recall how my mother always bought cookbooks and magazines with interesting recipes that she would try on the family. I really enjoyed helping her out in the kitchen. My mother would let me set the table and help cut out the homemade biscuits for breakfast. Sometimes she'd let me help her pick the mustard and turnip greens for our Sunday dinner.

I especially looked forward to the dinner parties. The New Year's Day dinner, in particular, was always a big "to do" in my house and it still is to this day. I enjoyed helping my mother make the deviled eggs and Swedish meatballs. We are now passing the torch to my daughter Kamaria who assists us both in the kitchen. She enjoys cooking as well.

At 6 years old, I can remember my mother encouraging me to make my first homemade pastry, a Hot Milk Sponge Cake. My whole family raved over how good it was, especially my mother. Boy, was I proud. From then on, I always wanted to cook something, and usually it was a dessert. My mother never scolded me for using her butter, sugar and flour. She still mentions that story from time to time.

When I was younger, my mother and father worked long hours during the week. So, on the weekends, my mother would cook enough food to last until Wednesday or Thursday. For those 2 or 3 days, my brother and I had to either eat can goods or learn how to cook. We chose the latter.

I can recall coming home from school and calling my mom to get instructions on how to prepare a dish for dinner. She would say, "Add a pinch of salt and a little pepper." I would ask, "How much is a pinch?" 'What do you mean when you say a little?" She would then instruct me on how to prepare the meal. I must say, she was a very good instructor, because somehow we were able to eat what I prepared.

Then, there is my grandmother Annie, who is 102 years old now. She was truly something in the kitchen. Family and friends would come from near and far to eat her cooking and no one could make dinner rolls like grandma. They were so tender; they would melt in your mouth.

Everyone loved her dinner rolls. Growing up I enjoyed spending the summers with her in Mississippi. She would take me fishing and make me go to the garden with her to gather vegetables and fruit to cook for dinner and can for the winter. I can still remember how sore my thumb would be from shelling fresh peas. I didn't enjoy doing it then, but oh how I appreciate those valuable lessons now. Grandma continued to cook and hand quilt until she was 97.

I also thank God for allowing me the honor of writing this book along with my sister and friend A'ishah. While growing up and even as an adult, I don't recall ever meeting anyone, my age, that enjoyed the art of cooking as much as I did until I met A'ishah. Whenever we came together, we would discuss recipes and exchange ideas for new dishes. About 7 years ago, I expressed to her that I was working on a cookbook and she shared with me that she was doing the same. So, we decided to join forces and write this cookbook for you. We hope you enjoy these creations as much as we do.

Savor the Flavor and Good Eating to you!

Kimberly

ABOUT THIS COOKBOOK

The authors of the cookbook, A'ishah T. Muhammad and Kimberly D. Muhammad are students in the Teachings of the **Most Honorable Elijah Muhammad** as taught by His National Representative, **The Honorable Minister Louis Farrakhan**. They are registered members in the Nation of Islam and students in the class of women and girls called the **M.G.T. and G.C.C.**

This was compiled out of love and concern for our sisters who have been asking us to share what we have been preparing through the years. It is not intended to be the definitive cookbook with the "perfect" recipes.

This cookbook is only intended to be a resource to help aspiring cooks and those who work diligently to put together healthy and wholesome meals at home for themselves and their families.

In using this cookbook, please note that butter as well as a butter substitute is mentioned in many recipes. You may use either, depending on your particular health requirements. However, we do advise to **not** substitute margarine for butter as it contains synthetic trans-fats which can drastically increase heart disease risks.

Regarding cooking oil, there are differing opinions as to which oil is best. Canola oil has become very popular in kitchens but it is not the healthiest choice. Corn oil and olive oil can and should be substituted for it in all of your recipes.

Whenever you have questions as to what is best to eat, we highly recommend the definitive books, **How To Eat To Live, Books I & II**, by the **Most Honorable Elijah Muhammad**.

How To Use This Cookbook

Welcome to the revised and digital version of **Coming Back Home: Recipes for Good Dining and Good Health**. This is the Kindle version of the cookbook so you won't wear out any pages on this version. Additionally, you will be able to make notes for each recipe on your tablet.

The **Key Ingredients** section of the cookbook was specifically configured to assist those who may be unfamiliar with them except in their processed and de-natured forms.

These herbs, fruits and vegetables are vital to the our diet in that they add nutrition, flavor and facilitate synergy to the recipes in this cookbook. In other words, just bring your cookbook with you as you shop for the key ingredients you need for your recipes.

If you are connected to the internet on your tablet, you will be able to touch hyperlinked pictures of these key Ingredients and be connected to the history and nutritional value for the ingredient as found on Wikipedia.

Future updates to the cookbook will include video and audio guides for some of the recipes and preparation needed to optimize your outcomes.

More than likely though you will find that you will be successful each and every time you try one of the wonderful recipes in this book.

We appreciate your purchase and would only ask you to share the news of it with your family, friends and loved ones and encourage them to obtain one for themselves.

Please rate us and give us your feedback that we may improve our book for your use.

Thanks again.

The Benefit of This Cookbook

(from a very reputable source)

"Coming Back Home is a staple cookbook in our home. (So much so that I'm almost ashamed to say that mine has been in pieces for the last few years; but that's how much use it gets!)

The recipe steps are so comprehensive that my girls have been cooking from this book since they were 9 years old!

There is no other mac n cheese recipe that we'll eat except this one. And the carrot pie recipe is perfection every time. The lemon pound cake has been hailed by one of our associates as part of his religion (smile). I can't say enough about this cookbook.

The carrot supreme is awesome; the Egyptian Cauliflower delicious; and of course the Navy Bean Soup is always a must when we have dinner guests.

I use this cookbook to make everything: soups and salads, entrees, breads, pies and desserts.

Coming Back Home is a must have for great dining, great health and all around great food!"

Staci Muhammad

Key Ingredients

acorn squash

allspice

asparagus

barley

basil

beets

black beans

blackberry

blueberry

brown lentils

brown rice

Brussels Sprout

13

butternut squash

cabbage

cardamon

chervil

chives

cilantro

cumin seed

dill

eggplant

garlic

green bell pepper

green onions

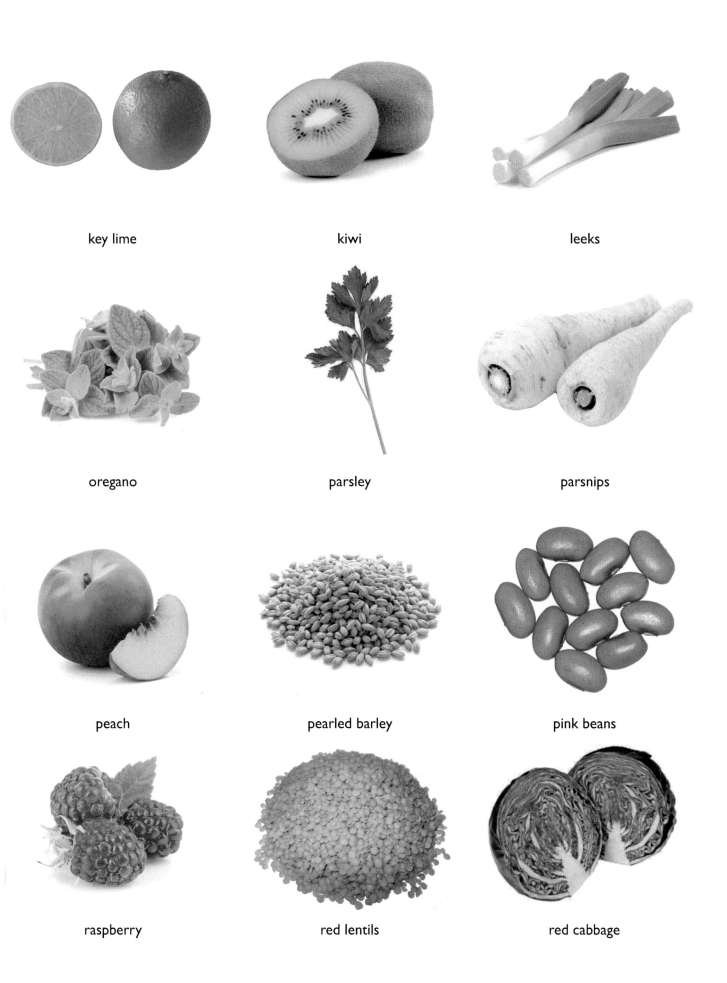

key lime

kiwi

leeks

oregano

parsley

parsnips

peach

pearled barley

pink beans

raspberry

red lentils

red cabbage

red onion

red potatoes

romaine lettuce

rutabaga

sage

spaghetti squash

spinach

sweet corn

sweet peas

cherry tomatoes

tamarind

thyme

Soups & Salads

VEGETABLE STOCK

1/3 cup olive oil

2 medium onions

2 carrots (scraped & chopped)

1 gallon water

1 leek (washed & chopped)

3 celery stalks with leaves (chopped)

5 plum tomatoes

2 parsnips (chopped)

5 garlic cloves (chopped)

8 sprigs parsley

5 allspice berries

10 black peppercorns

1 bay leaf

- In a large pot, put in olive oil, onions, garlic, celery, carrots, leek, and parsnips until vegetables are softened.

- Add plum tomatoes, parsley, bay leaf, pepper and one gallon of water.

- Simmer for 45 mins. on very low heat.

- Strain the stock, discard vegetables.

- Store in a tightly closed jar for up to four (4) days in refrigerator or freezer using zip-lock freezer bags or pour the cooled stock into ice cube trays, cover and freeze.

MAKING STOCK

Most soups depend upon stock to give them body, an because of this, stock is considered the primary source o a soup's consistency and flavor. With a little planning, yo can always have some homemade stock on hand.

Stock will keep in the refrigerator for only a few days bu it may be frozen for months.

Most of us are used to savory stock made by simmerin water for a period of time with meat and bones, seafoo and bones, or vegetables, along with the various herbs an spices that we may add.

However, the best stock which can be used in the wides variety of soups and sauces is a vegetable stock.

Making a vegetable stock eliminates the need in mos cases for straining or de-greasing as there is no meat o seafood by-products that require removal.

CREAM OF ASPARAGUS
& CAULIFLOWER SOUP

- In a large pot, combine oil, onion, garlic, celery and leek. Cook at medium heat until vegetables begin to soften.

- Add broth, potato, rosemary and thyme. Simmer for 15 minutes and add cauliflower. Cook for 15 minutes more.

- Remove cauliflower and puree. Add it back along with milk and asparagus, salt and pepper.

- Simmer for about 10 minutes and add parsley.

- Salt and pepper to taste.

1 leek (washed; sliced: white & light green part only)

1 cup olive oil

1 medium onion (chopped)

5 garlic cloves (chopped)

1 celery stalk (chopped)

4 cups vegetable broth

1 cauliflower (chopped)

2 small red potatoes

1 pinch of rosemary

½ lb. fresh asparagus

1½ cups milk

3 sprigs fresh parsley (chopped)

1 teaspoon dried thyme or 2 sprigs fresh thyme

Salt & pepper to taste

PINK BEAN WITH BARLEY SOUP

4 cups vegetable broth

4 cups cooked pink beans or 2 cans

of pink beans, rinsed

½ cup pearl barley

¼ cup olive oil

1 medium onion (chopped)

4 garlic cloves

1 celery stalk

½ cup leek (washed; sliced: white &

light green part only)

2 tablespoons sage

2 sprigs of thyme

Salt & pepper

- In a large pot, put in olive oil and heat on medium heat for about 30 seconds before adding onion, leek, garlic and celery. Cook until vegetables begin to soften.

- Add broth, beans and sage and bring to a simmer on medium heat for about 20 minutes. Stirring frequently to prevent scorching.

- Remove half of soup and place in a mixing bowl, puree (with hand blender wand or blender); being careful not to splatter hot liquid. Return pureed to remaining soup.

- Add barley, thyme, and pureed soup to bean soup and simmer for about an hour. Stir frequently. Salt and pepper to taste.

BLACK BEAN SOUP

- Sort beans and remove all debris (i.e. dirt, rocks, twigs). Rinse well in cold water. Place beans in a large bowl or stainless steel pot and cover with water. Add a dash of baking soda (1/8 teaspoon) and let soak 6-8 hours or overnight.

- Drain beans and rinse well in cold water. Place beans in a large pot (8-quart) with 2 quarts of cold water. Place pot on medium heat and bring beans to a boil (about 15 minutes).

- Sauté onions, peppers, celery and garlic in 1/8 cup of oil until tender.

- Add mixture to beans, reduce heat to low and cook until tender, approximately 50 minutes. Add remaining ingredients and cook another 20 minutes. Serve plain or with browned rice.

Chef's Tip: Garnish with scallions, shredded colby/jack cheese and/or sour cream. Accompanied by a tossed salad and whole-wheat rolls or jalapeño muffins, this makes for a great southwestern style meal.

2 cups black beans

3 tablespoons cumin

1 large onion (chopped)

2 tablespoons chili powder

1 medium bell pepper (chopped)

½ teaspoon cayenne pepper

3 stalks celery (chopped)

2 tablespoons sugar

1 garlic clove (minced)

1 teaspoon sea salt

¼ cup light olive oil

1 cup shredded carrots (optional)

1 tablespoon Italian seasoning

⅛ teaspoon baking soda

NAVY BEAN SOUP

1 lb. navy beans (sorted well & rinsed several times)

2 medium onions (chopped)

3 stalks celery (chopped)

1 green pepper (seeded & chopped)

4 garlic cloves (minced)

½ small can tomato paste

⅓ cup light olive oil

2 teaspoon paprika

1 tablespoon sugar

1 teaspoon sage (may substitute tumeric)

1 teaspoon salt

1 teaspoon ground pepper (cayenne may be substituted)

Water

* Optional - 2 large carrots (washed, peeled & chopped)

- Place rinsed beans in a large bowl or pot and cover with water overnight.

- (Quick-soak method: In a pot, partially cover beans with cold water and place over medium heat; bring to full boil for 3 minutes. Next, turn heat source off and leave beans covered for 2-3 hours then proceed to next step.)

- Drain beans and place in a large stainless steel pot. Add all ingredients except salt and tomato paste. (Doing so at this time prolongs cook time and keeps beans firmer than desired.)

- Cook beans over med-low heat; checking and stirring frequently until soft (approximately 3 hours).

- Add salt and tomato paste and stir until combined. Add hot water if soup if too thick and stir making sure beans do not stick.

- After beans have turned soft, put soup in a food mill and strain all ingredients.

- Salt to taste and serve.

COOKING HINT

You may opt to put your soup into a blender before pouring into the food mill.

First, put one cup of soup at a time into the blender and puree.

Be careful not to put more in a blender at a time or run the risk of being scalded by the extremely hot liquid.

VEGETABLE LENTIL SOUP

- In a medium soup pot, add oil over medium heat. Add onions, celery, carrots; garlic and bay leaf. Sauté until vegetables soften. Stir in curry powder; lower heat.

- Add lentils, crushed tomatoes, vegetable bouillon and water. Simmer over medium heat about 40 minutes. Stir occasionally to keep lentils from sticking to bottom. Remove bay leaf. Squeeze lemon juice then salt and pepper to taste.

- Ladle into bowls and serve with lemon wedge

3 tablespoons olive oil

1 onion (finely chopped)

2 celery stalks (finely chopped)

1 carrot (peeled and chopped)

10 garlic cloves (minced)

1 bay leaf

2 tablespoons vegetable bouillon seasoning

2 teaspoons curry powder

¾ cup red lentils (remove debris & sort)

1½ cups canned crushed tomatoes

5 cups water

½ lemon

Salt & pepper

FISH CHOWDER

1 lb. whiting fish fillets

1 cup shredded carrots

2 cups boiling water

2 tablespoons butter

1 lb. red potatoes (diced)

3 tablespoons unbleached flour

2 tablespoons olive oil

1 can evaporated milk

1 medium onion (finely chopped)

1 teaspoon salt

2 celery stalks (diced)

1/2 teaspoon pepper cayenne/white

1 red pepper (diced)

2 cups fresh/frozen corn

1 green pepper (diced)

1 bay leaf

2 garlic cloves (minced)

- Cut fish into bite size pieces. Place into boiling water and cook under medium heat until tender (approximately 10 minutes). Add potatoes to mixture.

- While fish is cooking, heat oil in a large skillet using medium heat. Add the onions, celery, peppers, garlic and carrots and cook covered until onions are tender and translucent (2-3 minutes), but not brown. Add to fish stock. Add corn to mixture and continue cooking.

- Melt butter in the skillet, add flour and stir until smooth. Slowly add milk a little at a time, stirring constantly to avoid lumps until all milk is used and the sauce has thickened. Add to fish and vegetable mixture and stir until well blended. Add salt, pepper and bay leaf. Reduce heat and continue cooking for 10 minutes. Make the chowder the day before serving so it will be full of flavor. Serves 6.

Chef's suggestion: Serve with a tossed salad and warm whole-wheat rolls or garlic/herb farina muffins.

EVERYTHING SALAD

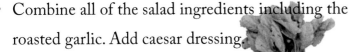

- Combine all of the salad ingredients including the roasted garlic. Add caesar dressing.

ROASTED GARLIC

- Cut garlic cloves in half and drizzle with ½ teaspoon olive oil. Roast in oven at 360° for approximately 10 minutes.

ROASTED BEETS W/ SALAD

- Wash and thoroughly scrape beets leaving just about inch of the beet tops in place. Blot dry with a paper towel

- Using a cutting board, slice beets about 1/8 inch thickness and place in Pyrex glass baking dish.

- Drizzle with olive oil and bake in a pre-heated 370 oven for approximately 15 minutes. Serve with salad.

CAESAR DRESSING

- Combine lemon juice, Worcestershire sauce and vinegar. Mix then add mustard, blend well. Drizzle in olive oil.

I bunch romaine lettuce (washed & patted dry)

½ small red onion (sliced)

½ cucumber (peeled & sliced)

½ pint grape tomatoes

I cup shredded red cabbage

½ red bell pepper (sliced thinly)

I cup broccoli florets (steamed)

4 garlic cloves

I carrot (shredded)

½ teaspoon olive oil

3 large beets

Caesar Dressing

2 tablespoons fresh lemon juice

2 teaspoons Worcestershire sauce

I teaspoon balsamic vinegar

2 teaspoon mustard (Grey Poupon© / French)

2 tablespoons olive oil

CARROT SUPREME
(NOT QUITE SALMON SALAD)

1 lb. carrots (washed & scraped)

2 tablespoons Bragg® Organic Coconut Liquid Aminos or worcestershire sauce

2 tablespoons sweet relish

½ cup finely chopped onion

½ cup finely chopped celery

½ cup finely chopped green pepper

½ cup mayonnaise

- Using a vegetable juicer, "juice" the carrots. (Only the pulp will be used in this recipe. You can drink the juice or it can be used at another time, but not in this recipe.)

- Using the pulp and the remaining ingredients, mix well and serve as you would salmon salad.

- Serve on bread or as an addition to a tossed salad.

CAULIFLOWER SALAD

- Break cauliflower into small pieces. Steam or cook in ½ cup water until tender. Drain and cool.

- In mixing bowl, add remaining ingredients. Add cauliflower and mix well. Sprinkle with paprika and refrigerate until cool.

- Serve as you would potato salad.

I head cauliflower (leaves discarded)

I small onion (finely chopped)

I stalk celery (chopped)

2 eggs (boiled and chopped)

¼ cup sweet pickle relish

Mayonnaise

I tablespoon yellow mustard

I teaspoon garlic powder

I teaspoon onion powder

¼ teaspoon ground pepper or a pinch of cayenne

Paprika

MY CHOPPED SALAD

1 cup frozen green sweet peas (thawed)

1 carrot (peeled & chopped)

½ red onion (chopped)

1 cucumber (peeled & chopped)

½ cup sweet corn

1 cup red cabbage

½ cup parsley (chopped)

1 cup grape tomatoes (cut in half)

2 garlic cloves (minced)

3 romaine lettuce leaves (chopped)

1 small green bell pepper (chopped)

½ cup mayonnaise

½ cup italian dressing

½ cup black beans (cooked) (* optional - green lentils or navy beans)

• Combine all ingredients and refrigerate until ready to serve.

A'ISHAH'S PERSONAL NOTE

This is a salad that I grew up eating in New Jersey. I thought everybody ate it because it was so common for my family. I came to find out that this sald was quite uncommon, in fact and do I have made a few adjustments to suit my tastes. Now I love it and my guests rave about this seemingly simple combination.

Éntrées & Side Dishes

EGGPLANT CASSEROLE

1 medium eggplant

2 medium onions (sliced)

2 medium tomatoes (sliced)

½ cup vegetable oil

3 tablespoons flour

½ cup grated Parmesan cheese

1 tablespoon onion powder

2 low sodium vegetable bouillon cubes

Cayenne, salt & pepper

1 can evaporated milk

2 cups Uncle Ben's Converted Rice

- Wash and slice eggplant leaving skin on. Lightly salt slices and cover with a heavy plate for at least 10 minu (to remove bitterness). Wipe off salt then dip slices in milk and dredge in flour.

- In oiled pan, lightly brown eggplant on both sides. Se aside and save 3 tablespoons oil for remaining portion recipe.

- Heat oven to 370° and place 2 cups of rice on cookie sheet. Brown for about 15 minutes before removing fr oven. (Leave oven on.) Rinse in colander until water runs clear.

- Place rice in pot with 1 tablespoon of oil, 1 bouillon cube, a pinch of salt and 4 cups of water. Cover and simmer until water has been absorbed. Set aside.

- In a heated saucepan with 2 tablespoons of oil, heat onion slices until softened. Add 3 tablespoons of flour and stir. Add evaporated milk, 1 bouillon cube, onion powder, Parmesan cheese, a pinch of cayenne pepper, s and black pepper. Simmer until sauce coats back of spoon. Set aside.

- In a Pyrex dish, layer rice, eggplant and tomatoes. Repeat layering; ending with rice.

- Pour gravy over casserole and bake at 370º for 50 minutes.

CABBAGE - CARROT STRUDEL

- Heat oven to 375°. In skillet, melt 1 tablespoon butter or butter substitute and 2 tablespoons of olive oil. Add carrots, cabbage, garlic, onions, Swiss Formula Broth and seasoning salt. Cook until softened. Remove from heat, stir in dill, and oat bran.

- Melt remaining butter or butter substitute and set aside.

- Lay open 1 phyllo sheet and using a pastry brush, spread on it 1 tablespoon of melted butter or butter substitute and lightly sprinkle feta cheese.

- Repeat the above with the next 8-10 layers (phyllo sheets).

- With last layer (sheet), use remaining butter or butter substitute, and feta cheese. Then add cabbage/carrot mixture, fold both sides similar to how you'd seal an envelope and then roll-up. (This can be a bit messy initially until you get the hang of it.)

- Place roll, seam side down in baking dish. Brush roll with any remaining butter or butter substitute or olive oil. Place extra phyllo sheets over the roll and tuck neatly. Repeat and end by brushing on butter or butter substitute.

- Bake in oven for 40 minutes.

- Let cool for at least 15 minutes before slicing. Serves 6.

¾ cup butter or butter substitute

1 cup olive oil

3 cups cabbage (chopped/shredded)

2 medium carrots (scrapped & chopped)

1 onion (chopped)

2 garlic cloves (chopped)

1 tablespoon dill

1 tablespoon seasoning salt

2 tablespoons All Natural Vegetable bouillon

4 oz. feta cheese w/ basil

¾ cup oat bran

1 roll phyllo dough sheets (*thawed: sold in frozen foods section, not to be confused with pastry puff*)

VEGETABLE MOUSSAKA

1 lb. eggplant (washed & sliced with skin on)

1 cup sweet green peas or cooked lentils (drained)

¼ cup olive oil

3 garlic cloves (crushed)

1 14 ozs. can chopped/crushed tomatoes in puree

2 tablespoon Vegetable bouillon seasoning

1 teaspoon seasoning salt

4 medium potatoes (peeled and sliced)

Béchamel Sauce

4 tablespoons butter or butter substitute

1 ½ cup low-fat milk

3 tablespoons unbleached flour

¼ teaspoon grated nutmeg

½ cup plain yogurt

1 tablespoon Vegetable bouillon seasoning mix

Salt & pepper

Pinch cayenne pepper

**½ cup cheddar cheese (grated) optional

- Preheat oven to 365 ° F. Sprinkle the eggplant slices with salt and place a heavy plate on top. Let sit at least 20 minutes and allow juices to be extracted. Drain. Boil potatoes in salted water until tender, drain.

- Heat 2 tablespoons oil in pan, add onion, garlic, green peas, tomatoes, seasoning salt, and Vegetable bouillon seasoning; simmer, stirring occasionally. Salt to taste.

- Rinse eggplant slices, pat dry. Use remaining oil in a skillet and cook the slices until slightly browned on both sides. Drain on paper towels.

- In a baking dish, arrange a layer of eggplant, then a layer of sliced potatoes, then tomato mixture. Repeat layering until eggplant slices and tomato mixture is used.

Béchamel Sauce

- Melt butter in sauce pan. Add flour and stir. Slowly add milk, yogurt and remaining ingredients and heat slowly until sauce thickens slightly, stir frequently. Add salt and pepper to taste.

- Pour over eggplant/potato casserole. Sprinkle cheese generously and bake 45 minutes until top is golden but not too brown.

- Remove from oven and let sit for about 10 minutes before serving.

EGGPLANT PARMESAN

- Peel eggplant and slice it into inches.

- In a plastic bag, place bread crumbs and oregano. Mix eggs with 2 tablespoons of water in a bowl. Using a paper towel, wipe off and pat dry each piece of eggplant before dipping in egg mixture. Take the dipped slice of eggplant into the bag with bread crumbs and shake to dredge.

- Heat a pan with olive oil until hot but not smoking. Lightly brown on each side, then drain on paper bag or paper towels. Repeat until all of the eggplant slices are cooked.

- In a Pyrex baking dish, line bottom with eggplant, then garlic, then cheese. Repeat until eggplant is completely layered. In a sauté pan, sauté onion, red bell pepper, carrot, Italian seasoning, 1 teaspoon sugar, 1 can tomatoes in puree, salt and pepper. Simmer and stir for 10 minutes. Pour prepared tomato sauce on top and sides of eggplant.

- Sprinkle with remaining shredded cheese and Parmesan. Bake at 365° for 40 minutes. Remove from oven and let sit 10 minutes to set before serving.

Note: If you desire a crispier eggplant, first dip eggplant slice in flour, then egg, then bread crumbs before browning. Also, lessen amount of sauce you pour on when baking.

2 medium eggplants (peeled & sliced)

½ cup olive oil

I large onion (sliced)

I medium red bell pepper

I carrot (scrapped and chopped)

8 garlic cloves (sliced)

I cup bread crumbs, cracker meal or whole wheat flour

I tablespoon Italian Seasoning

2 eggs beaten or 4 egg whites

¾ cup shredded low-fat mozzarella

I large can tomatoes (pureed)

I teaspoon sugar

Salt and pepper

HELPFUL HINT

Set eggplant on a plate and sprinkle with salt. Place a heavy plate on top of eggplant and let sit about 20 mins. This helps remove bitter taste and keeps eggplant from absorbing too much oil.

Including a carrot in the sauce helps to balance the acidity of the tomatoes and gives a slight sweetness as well.

EGGPLANT PARMESAN
(LOW-FAT)

I large eggplant

8 ozs. (2 cups) shredded low-fat

mozzarella cheese

I teaspoon each salt / pepper

Olive or light olive oil

½ cup grated Parmesan cheese

I teaspoon dried basil leaves

16 ozs. spaghetti sauce (2 Cups)

I teaspoon dried oregano leaves

- Preheat oven to 375 degrees.

- Cut eggplant into inch slices; sprinkle with salt and pepper on both sides; place on broiler pan. Brush with oil. Broil.

- When top side is browned, turn it over (using a flat edged spatula), brush other side with oil and brown. Pour 1/3 of spaghetti sauce in bottom of greased 9x13x2 inch baking pan. Place half of eggplant slices in single layer in baking pan. Sprinkle with half of basil, oregano, mozzarella and Parmesan cheeses.

- Pour another 1/3 of spaghetti sauce over layers in pan. Repeat eggplant, herbs, sauce and cheese layers. Bake 35 to 40 minutes. Serves 9.

- This dish may also be prepared by dipping seasoned eggplant slices in an egg/milk mixture, coat with whole wheat flour and pan fry in oil until lightly browned on both sides. Drain slices on paper towel and proceed with layering sauce, herbs and cheeses and bake.

Chef's Tip: Vegetable soup, tossed salad and garlic wheat toast compliments this entrée well.

KIM'S MACARONI AND CHEESE

- Preheat oven to 350° F. Butter a 1 quart casserole dish. Boil macaroni according to package directions; drain and rinse in cold water.

- In a medium saucepan, over low heat, melt 2 tablespoons of butter. Blend in flour, stirring constantly. Gradually stir in milk and cream. Cook stirring constantly, until mixture begins to boil and thicken (2-3 minutes). Add 1/2 cup of cheese and continue stirring until cheese is melted. Remove from heat and add salt and pepper to taste.

- In a small bowl or teacup, beat egg with a fork. Add beaten egg to mixture stirring constantly until well blended. Set aside.

- Put half of the macaroni in the buttered dish. Sprinkle with half of the cheese. Add the remaining macaroni and top with the remaining cheese. Pour mixture over layered macaroni and cheese and dot with additional butter. Sprinkle with paprika. Bake 25 to 30 minutes until bubbly and golden brown on top.

- Serves 4 to 6.

1½ cups elbow macaroni

1 large nest egg

4 tablespoons butter

½ teaspoon salt or to taste

2 tablespoons unbleached flour

½ teaspoon white pepper

¼ cup milk

2½ cups grated sharp cheese

1 cup light cream

Paprika

CANDIED CARROTS

I lb. carrots (scraped and cut into ¼ inch slices) or baby carrots

¾ cup sugar (turbinado or white)

¼ cup butter

I teaspoon nutmeg

½ teaspoon cinnamon

I teaspoon vanilla

Dash of salt

- In a medium saucepan, add 3 cups of water and salt; bring to a rolling boil.

- Scrape carrots and cut off the tips and ends. Slice carrots diagonally into ¼ inch pieces. (If using baby carrots, just rinse and add to boiling water.) Add carrots to water and bring to a boil. Reduce heat and continue cooking carrots until tender (approximately 10 minutes).

- Drain carrots and add remaining ingredients. Continue cooking under medium heat until sugar and butter melts and has the consistency of light syrup. Remove from heat. Serves 4.

One medium butternut squash (cut into 1 inch pieces) may be substituted for carrots.

For a little zing, add 1/2 teaspoon of orange zest or 1/4 cup orange or pineapple juice after carrots are tender.

RUTABAGA

- Place rutabaga, carrot, onion, onion powder and bouillon cubes in a sauce pan and add enough water to almost cover the vegetables.

- Partially cover and simmer over medium heat for about 45 minutes or until rutabaga is tender.

- Drain and add butter and parsley.

- Mash partially and add salt and pepper to taste.

Comments

A'ishah: "When I was a young girl, I thought this rutabaga (we called them turnips) was a hot vegetable. I later learned that my father had a heavy hand when it came to using black pepper."

1 medium rutabaga (cut in quarters & peeled)

1 carrot (peeled & chopped)

1 onion (peeled & cut in half)

1 tablespoon onion powder

1 teaspoon parsley flakes

2 vegetable bouillon cubes

1 tablespoon olive oil

1 tablespoon butter

Salt and pepper

EGYPTIAN CAULIFLOWER

1 cauliflower (leaves discarded

& cut into florets

2 eggs or 4 egg whites

2 tablespoon water

1 onion (sliced)

1 bell pepper (seeded & sliced)

2 garlic cloves (minced)

¼ teaspoon salt and pepper

2 cups tomato sauce (marinara

or spaghetti)

¼ cup olive oil or light olive oil

- Preheat oven to 365° F.

- Beat eggs, water, salt and pepper. Dip cauliflower florets in mixture and coat well.

- In a skillet, heat oil over medium-low heat. Add cauliflower being careful not to crowd.

- Turn to brown lightly on all sides. Drain on paper-towels or brown paper bag.

- Place cauliflower, onion, green pepper and garlic in Pyrex baking dish. Cover with sauce and bake for 20 minutes.

- Serve with brown rice.

You may opt to place battered cauliflower in a Pyrex baking dish then lightly drizzle with olive oil. Bake at 365° oven until tender, turning it. Add tomato sauce, onion, green bell pepper and garlic to cauliflower on top. Return to oven and bake 20 minutes. Serve.

RED FISH CURRY

- Place the fish on a plate and rub over with the curry powder and salt.

- Heat 3 tablespoons of oil in a large frying pan until hot. Lightly dust fish pieces with flour and add to the oil. Cook until fish is lightly browned, about 1 minute, turning once. Do not fully cook fish. Remove fish to the plate.

- To the same pan, add onions, garlic, red pepper, mustard, and curry leaves; cook about 3 minutes until the onions are soft, .

- Stir in the water, tomatoes, and tamarind and bring to a boil. Simmer about 8 minutes until the sauce is reduced and thickened.

- Gently slip in the fish and the accumulated juices. Cook until the fish is heated through about 2 minutes. Garnish with cilantro leaves.

Note: To make garam masala, combine coriander, fenugreek, mustard, cumin, black pepper, fennel, cinnamon, cloves, grind a fine powder using an electric grinder. Stir in the turmeric and red pepper and transfer into a jar. Cover tightly and keep in a cool place.

1½ lbs. skinless/boneless non-oily fish fillets (cut into 4 serving pieces)

1 tablespoon curry powder or garam masala

½ cup unbleached flour

Coarse salt

3 tablespoons olive oil

½ onion (finely chopped)

4 garlic cloves (chopped)

1 tablespoon ground cumin

½ tablespoon ground coriander

½ tablespoon paprika

¼ cup vegetable bouillon cube

1 teaspoon mustard powder

12 kari leaves or 2 bay leaves

1½ cups water

½ lb. of plum tomatoes (chopped)

¼ cup tamarind water or 1 tablespoon tamarind paste (dissolved in ¼ cup of hot paper)*

Cilantro Sprigs for garnish

PEPPY FISH SAUSAGE

1 lb. whiting fillets (skin removed)

2 tablespoons rubbed sage

2 teaspoon rubbed thyme

1 teaspoon garlic salt (or garlic powder plus 1 teaspoon salt)

½ teaspoon crushed red pepper flakes

1 tablespoon olive oil

3 tablespoons butter (or butter substitute)

- Cut whiting fillets into small pieces and place in food processor a little at a time. Remove and place in a stainless steel bowl until all the fish is minced. Add remaining ingredients except butter to minced fish. Remove and place in a bowl.

- Put butter (1 tablespoon at a time) into skillet and melt on low-medium heat.

- With clean hands shape fish mixture into small patties. Place in skillet and brown on both sides.

- Serve with your favorite breakfast food (waffles, eggs and potatoes).

Comments

A'ishah: "When I finally figured out how to prepare this I was a new bride. When my husband came home, I plopped a piece into his mouth before he could protest. For a brief second, he thought I had given him a forbidden food (pork) before I happily exclaimed, 'It's fish sausage! I did it! I did it!'"

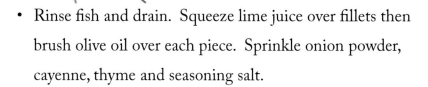

BARBECUED FISH

- Rinse fish and drain. Squeeze lime juice over fillets then brush olive oil over each piece. Sprinkle onion powder, cayenne, thyme and seasoning salt.

- Liberally place onion, celery, garlic and bell pepper over each fillets. Pour barbecue sauce over fillets.

- In a preheated 365° oven, cover fish and cook for 20 minutes or until fish flakes easily.

- Serve with cauliflower salad.

I lb. fish fillets (whiting w/ scales removed)

I onion (chopped)

5 garlic cloves (minced

½ cup green bell pepper (chopped)

½ lime (room temp.)

I tablespoon onion powder

¼ teaspoon cayenne pepper or chili powder

I teaspoon thyme (ground)

½ seasoning salt

¾ cup barbecue sauce

3 tablespoon olive oil

FISH PUNJABI

1 lb. white fish (or orange roughy) fillets skinned

2 onions (sliced)

4 garlic cloves (minced)

1 teaspoon ginger

1 tablespoon curry powder

1 teaspoon ground cumin

1½ ground cinnamon

1½ teaspoon ground coriander

Pinch of cayenne pepper

5 cardamoms (pods-crushed)

2 tablespoons Vegetable bouillon seasoning

3 tablespoons butter or light olive oil

3 cans canned crushed tomatoes

½ cup light cream or half & half

1 tablespoon lemon juice

3 sprigs cilantro (wash & chopped)

Salt

- Heat butter in a pan and add onions until golden. In the meantime, put ginger and garlic in a blender with about ¼ cup water and pulse to blend for 1-2 minutes.

- Add garlic/ginger paste to onions along with ground coriander, cumin, curry, cinnamon, cayenne, cardamom and vegetable bouillon. Simmer for 2 minutes, add pinch of salt.

- Stir in tomatoes, cream and lemon juice. Simmer on low for 5-6 minutes. Mixture will thicken slightly. Be careful not to overcook or mixture will separate.

- Make sure fish is drained and pat dry. Add to tomato mixture and simmer on low until tender (10-15 minutes).

- Sprinkle with chopped cilantro and serve.

BEST BURGERS
(VEGETARIAN)

- Sauté green peppers, onions, celery in 1 tablespoon of oil for 2 minutes.

- Mix vegetables, brown rice, egg whites, farina, oatmeal, wheat germ, steak sauce, Worcestershire sauce, and seasoning salt.

- Shape mixture into burgers (not too thick), dredge in wheat flour and place in hot oiled skillet for about 2 minutes each side until browned. Drain.

- Serve on burger buns with all the fixings or simply smother with gravy and serve with vegetables and brown rice.

½ green bell pepper (chopped)

½ small onion (chopped)

½ celery stalk (chopped)

1 tablespoon oil (light olive, corn or light olive)

1 cup Farina® or Malto Meal® (uncooked)

½ cup oatmeal

¾ cup wheat germ

2 tablespoons steak sauce

1 tablespoon salt or seasoning salt

1 cup whole wheat flour

2 tablespoons Worcestershire Sauce (low sodium)

1 cup vegetables (chopped broccoli, carrots, etc.)

2 cups brown rice (prepared according to directions with the following)

2 tablespoons All Natural Vegetable bouillon

2 egg whites (or Egg Beaters® equivalent)

VEGETARIAN CHILI

2 cups lentils or small pink beans

5 tablespoons chili powder or to taste

I large onion (chopped)

¼ - ½ teaspoon cayenne pepper

I medium bell pepper (green, red or yellow / chopped)

I teaspoon sea salt

I tablespoon sugar

3 stalks celery (chopped)

I clove garlic (minced)

¼ cup light olive oil

I tablespoon Italian seasoning

I tablespoon cumin

I cup browned rice (optional)

2 cups fresh diced tomatoes or I - 14 1/2 oz. can diced or crushed tomatoes or tomato sauce

I cup shredded carrots or sliced squash (zucchini or yellow, optional)

⅛ teaspoon baking soda

- Sort beans and remove all debris (i.e. dirt, rocks, twigs). If using the small pink beans, after rinsing, place beans in a large bowl or pot and cover with cold water.

- Add a dash of baking soda (⅛ teaspoon), stir and let pink beans soak for 6-8 hours. Before cooking, drain and rinse beans thoroughly under cold water and place in a large stainless steel pot with 2 quarts of water. Place pot on medium heat and bring beans to a boil.

- While beans are cooking, heat oil in skillet or Dutch oven until hot. Add onions, garlic, celery and bell peppers to oil. In ⅛ cup oil, sauté until tender or until onions are translucent.

- Add sautéed vegetables, herbs, spices and remaining oil to beans, stir well. Cover with lid and cook until beans are slightly tender, approximately 30 minutes. Add rice (if cooking lentils) and stir well.

- Bring mixture to a boil, cover and reduce heat to low and cook until rice is almost done (approximately 15 minutes).

- Add remaining ingredients, stir well and continue cooking for 15 minutes or until done. Add more seasoning to taste if needed.

Chef's Tip: Garnish with shredded cheese, chopped onions, sour cream and/or jalapeños. Coupled with jalapeño or cheese muffins, a tossed salad and Iced tea, you'll have a delicious, hearty meal in just 60 minutes. Makes 12 servings, 1 cup each.

LENTIL LOAF

- Sort beans and remove all debris. Pour lentils into a 3-quart saucepan and cover with water, so that the water is double the height of the lentils. Bring to a boil and cook on medium heat for 30 minutes, or until they are tender. Drain lentils to remove excess liquid and cool.

- Preheat oven to 375 degrees. Oil a 9x5x3 inch loaf pan. Set aside.

- Process lentils in a food mill or food processor. Heat oil in skillet or frying pan over medium heat and saute' onions and garlic until onions are translucent. Add celery, green peppers and carrots and continue cooking until the vegetables are soft.

- In a large bowl, mix the sautéed vegetables and oil, pureed lentils, half of bread crumbs (¾ cup) and flour. Season with parsley, salt, pepper and thyme. Mix well.

- Add eggs and mix well (I prefer using my clean hands for this part). Add more bread crumbs (¼ cup at a time) to mixture until texture soft but not sticky.

- Pat mixture into loaf pan. Bake uncovered 30-35 minutes until a knife inserted in center comes out clean. Serves 6.

Chef's Tip: Serve with mashed, roasted or new potatoes or brown rice and fresh steamed green beans or broccoli with sweet red peppers. For extra flavor, serve with a tangy tomato sauce.

2 cups lentil beans

2 eggs (beaten well)

1 medium onion (diced)

1½ - 2 cups bread crumbs

1 clove garlic (minced)

½ cup whole-wheat flour

2 stalks celery (diced)

2 teaspoons fresh parsley (chopped)

1 medium green pepper (chopped)

1½ teaspoon salt

2 carrots (grated)

½ teaspoon ground white pepper

¼ cup light olive oil

¼ teaspoon fresh thyme

TANGY TOMATO GLAZE

3/4 cup ketchup

1/4 teaspoon mustard

2 tablespoons brown sugar

1/4 teaspoon white pepper

In a small bowl or cup, mix ingredients well and pour and spread over the top of loaf for the last 15 minutes of cooking time. Lentil loaf never tasted so good.

HOMESTYLE GRAVY

3 tablespoons light olive oil

1 medium onion (chopped / sliced)

3 garlic cloves (minced)

2 tablespoons unbleached flour

2 Rapunzle© vegetarian cubes

1 cups water

Pinch of cayenne pepper

1 tablespoon Worcestershire sauce

teaspoon Liquid Smoke©

Salt & pepper

- Sauté the onion in the oil for about 10 minutes until it softens then add garlic and stir for about 30 seconds.

- Add the flour and stir to reduce "raw" taste of flour.

- Add remaining ingredients and simmer on low for about 10 minutes.

- If gravy is too thick, add a little water until desired consistency is reached.

SPINACH QUICHE

PIE CRUST

- Combine all pastry ingredients and shape into a ball. If too dry, add 1/8 teaspoon of cold water and work in without too much handling. Refrigerate for 20 minutes.

FILLING

- In a sauté pan, heat spinach, along with the onion until slightly wilted. Drain well and squeeze.

- Using a food processor or blender, add remaining ingredients and puree for about 30 seconds.

- Remove pastry from refrigerator. Place on floured surface and roll flat starting and returning to the center extending away until a circular shape emerges. Using your rolling pin, partially roll pastry up on it in order to transfer to a pie or baking dish.

- Remove rolling pin, trim excess dough around edge, pinch edges or prick with a fork.

- Pour filling into prepared pastry crust to the top without overfilling.

- Bake at 360° for 40 minutes. Remove from oven and let *rest at least 10 minutes cutting.*

Note: Allowing the quiche to rest before cutting keeps the hot filling from running out after it is sliced.

PIE CRUST

6 tablespoons butter or butter substitute (room temp.)

¾ cup whole wheat flour (plus extra for rolling and shaping the pie crust).

¼ cup wheat germ

Pinch of salt

¼ cup cold water

FILLING

1 10 oz. box frozen spinach

1 medium chopped onion

2 eggs or 3 egg whites

1 can evaporated milk

2 tablespoon butter or butter substitute

¼ cup mayonnaise

½ cup shredded cheese (swiss, cheddar or "rice-bran"[no soy])

1 tablespoon seasoning salt

Pinch of cayenne pepper

EGG ROLLS

4 tablespoons light olive oil

1 teaspoon sugar

½ teaspoon minced garlic

½ teaspoon white pepper

1 large cabbage (approx. 1 ½ pounds)

12 egg roll wrappers

1 cup shredded carrots

1 teaspoon soy sauce

¼ teaspoon Chinese 5 Spice or 1/8 teaspoon fresh ginger

1 small onion (finely chopped) or 3 green onions (sliced)

1 tablespoon corn starch (blended with 2 tablespoons cold water)

- Cut cabbage into quarters, trim off and discard the core at the point of each quarter. Rinse, drain and set aside. Peel carrots, rinse and drain. In a large bowl, grate cabbage and carrots.

- Heat 2 tablespoons oil in large frying pan under medium heat. Saut onion and garlic until onion is translucent. Add cabbage and carrots to the onion/garlic mixture.

- Cook uncovered, stirring occasionally for 5 to 7 minutes, or until the vegetables are crisp-tender. Add soy sauce, seasoning and sugar. Mix well. Remove from heat and let mixture cool.

- Place a tablespoon of mixture in the middle of an egg roll wrapper on diagonal. Fold bottom corner up, left corner in and right corner in. Brush edge of remaining corner with cornstarch mixture, then fold to seal. Continue this way until all wrappers are used up.

- Heat remaining oil in a large wok or deep fryer and fry egg rolls for approximately 3-4 minutes each side until golden. Drain on paper towels and keep warm until serving.sauce over mixture. Sprinkle with remaining cheese.

BROCCOLI CASSEROLE

- Preheat oven to 350 degrees and cook rice according to package directions.

- Trim the leaves and course stems ends from the broccoli, and cut the remaining stems and florets into bite-size pieces. Wash thoroughly. In a 2-quart saucepan, bring 1 cup salted water to a boil. Add broccoli, cover and boil for 5 minutes or until crisp tender. Drain thoroughly in a colander and transfer to a buttered 2-quart casserole dish.

- Melt stick of butter in a 1-quart saucepan over medium heat. Add onion and cook, uncovered until transparent. Add flour, salt, pepper and thyme and stir until smooth. Continue cooking and stirring until mixture boils and thickens (about 5 minutes).

- Gradually add milk and a cup of cheddar cheese to mixture and continue cooking over medium heat until smooth. Remove from heat.

- Combine the cooked broccoli and rice in large bowl and mix well. Transfer broccoli and rice into buttered dish. Pour cream sauce over mixture. Sprinkle with remaining cheese.

- Melt ½ stick butter in small saucepan. Add bread crumbs and blend well. Place bread crumb mixture over casserole, pat down if necessary. Sprinkle with Paprika and bake uncovered for 30 minutes. Serves 8-10

Chef's Tips: Cauliflower may be substituted for broccoli or combine them. Cook the rice in vegetarian (not chicken broth) instead of water for that extra special flavor (my favorite).

1 large head broccoli

2 cups milk

½ stick butter

1½ cups cooked brown rice

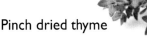

1 small finely chopped onion

1 cup bread crumbs

3 tablespoons unbleached flour

½ teaspoon salt

1½ cup cheddar cheese

½ teaspoon pepper

Paprika

Pinch dried thyme

SPAGHETTI SQUASH

1 medium yellow spaghetti squash

TOMATO SAUCE

2 onions (diced)

1 carrot (peeled & chopped)

15 garlic cloves (minced)

1/3 cup celery (chopped)

1/3 cup olive oil

2 tomatoes (chopped)

1 28 oz. can of tomato purée

½ cup water

1½ teaspoon sugar

2 tablespoon grated Parmesan or Romano cheese

1 tablespoon basil

2 tablespoon Italian Seasoning

Salt & Pepper

SPAGHETTI SQUASH

- Cut squash lengthwise. Scoop out seeds and place flat side down in a baking dish with 1½ cup water.

- Cover and bake for about 50 minutes in a 375° oven.

- Squash is done when outer skin is easily pierced with fork. Remove from baking dish and let cool a few minutes.

- Scrape out "strands" of squash with fork. Discard shells. Serve with tomato sauce.

TOMATO SAUCE

- Sauté onions, carrot, celery, garlic, and olive oil.

- After 10 minutes, add tomatoes, tomato purée and water and let simmer for a half hour

- Simmer another 20 minutes on low, stirring periodically.

- Add sugar, grated cheese, basil, and Italian Seasoning

- Add chopped parsley towards last 10 minutes of cooking time.

- Salt and pepper to taste.

Comments

A'ishah: "My mom used to prepare this when it was hardly heard of. This gourd is becoming increasingly more popular and can be found in just about every grocery store."

EASY STOVE TOP WHITE FISH

- In a large skillet, heat oil on low.

- Add onions, garlic, green pepper, carrots and stir around until vegetables begin to soften.

- Add tomato sauce, italian seasoning, thyme, sugar, salt and pepper. Let simmer on low for 4 minutes.

- Place fillets on top and cover. Simmer for about 4 minutes or until fish is done. Sprinkle lemon juice on top and serve alone or over rice. Serves 4.

Comments

A'ishah: "This dish is so easy to prepare that it could practically be done while your family is walking in the door and be completed by the time they wash their hands and sit down to the table."

4 White Fish fillets

1 C prepared tomato sauce or crushed tomatoes

1 medium onion (sliced into rings)

1 small green pepper (seeded & sliced)

3 garlic cloves (minced)

Olive oil

1 carrot (peeled & sliced on angle)

Italian seasoning

¼ t thyme (fresh or ground)

Salt & pepper

Pinch of sugar

1 t fresh lemon juice

BROWN STEW FISH

2 lbs. red snapper (head on; gutted & scaled w/ fins clipped)

1 onion (sliced into rings)

½ C chopped bell pepper (seeded)

2 Scallions (chopped)

2 T Worcestershire sauce

2 sprigs fresh thyme

1 T butter

½ teaspoon of jerk seasoning sauce

½ C water

2 T olive oil

2 T Ketchup

¼ C unbleached flour / 1 T unbleached flour

- Heat a skillet on a medium flame; adding 2 tablespoons olive oil.

- Wash and pat dry fish with paper towel. Sprinkle inside and out with salt & pepper. Lightly coat the outside with flour (¼ cup of flour) and place in skillet. Carefully brown each side.

- Remove fish from skillet and place on plate.

- In same skillet, add onion until it softens.

- Add flour (1 T flour) until browned; add the rest of the ingredients; mix well and let simmer.

- Return fish to pot and simmer for another 15 minutes. Salt & pepper to taste. Serves 2.

Comments

A'ishah: "Growing up on the East Coast, there are a lot of Caribbean influences. This is one of my favorite dishes especially served with smothered cabbage and plantains."

SAUTÉED BROCCOLINI

- Wash broccolini and cut bunch in half.

- Place in 1½ cup boiling salted water for 2 minutes. Remove from heat and drain.

- Submerge broccolini in ice water for about 30 seconds and drain again.

- Heat a skillet with olive oil over medium heat. Place broccolini in hot pan. Add garlic and celery. Stir fry until garlic softens. Add scallions and stir.

- Remove from heat and serve.

I bunch broccolini

3 garlic cloves (chopped)

I scallion (green onion) chopped)

½ celery stalk (chopped)

Olive oil

Salt

Water

CAULIFLOWER
(In Cream Sauce)

I cauliflower (leaves & stem removed)

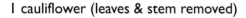

4 garlic cloves (minced)

I teaspoon turmeric

I vegetable bouillon cube

I cup milk

I tablespoon flour

2 tablespoons butter

I teaspoon onion powder

Pinch of nutmeg

Salt

Pinch of cayenne pepper

Parsley flakes

- Break cauliflower into florets and place in boiling salted water. Simmer over medium heat until just tender. Remove and drain. Keep warm.

- In a sauce pan, melt the butter. Add garlic and flour then add bouillon, tumeric, onion powder, nutmeg, cayenne and milk. Turn heat to low and be careful not to scorch mixture.

- Add milk and whisk constantly until sauce thickens. Salt to taste.

- Place cauliflower in warm serving bowl and pour sauce over it. Sprinkle parsley leaves on top and serve immediately.

- Serves 4.

BAIGAN BHARTA

(Indian Style Eggplant)

- In a sauce pan, heat oil and add eggplant. Stir until softened. Remove eggplant from pan and set aside.

- To the pan, add onions and cook until softened. Add garlic, Vegetable bouillon, curry powder, paprika, chili powder, and turmeric; stir to combine.

- Add tomatoes and lime juice. Add sautéed eggplant and stir over low-medium heat. Sauce will cook down and eggplant will begin to puree. Salt to taste.

- Garnish with chopped cilantro leaves and serve with rice.

1 large eggplant (peeled & cubed)

2 onions (chopped)

1 10 oz. can crushed tomatoes

4 garlic cloves (minced)

2 tablespoons lime juice

2 tablespoons olive oil

1 tablespoon Vegetable bouillon Mix

1 teaspoon curry powder

1 teaspoon paprika

¼ teaspoon chili powder

½ teaspoon turmeric

Cilantro leaves

Salt

MAPLE GLAZED BRUSSELS SPROUTS

1 lb. Brussels sprouts (halved thru the stem)

3 garlic cloves (minced)

2½ tablespoon olive oil

1½ tablespoon maple syrup

1 teaspoon fresh thyme leaves

¼ cup water

Salt & pepper to taste

- Heat a large skillet over medium heat. Add the olive oil and Brussels sprouts. As Brussels sprouts begin to cook, add garlic. Sprinkle with the salt and pepper. Stir until vegetables begin to turn brown.

- Add the water and cook until tender but not too soft. Add thyme leaves.

- Add syrup and lemon juice and stir. Remove from heat and serve.

Comments

A'ishah: "My daughter was not a fan of Brussels sprouts, like most, until I prepared them in this way. Now, she requests them. Imagine that."

CANDIED CARROTS

- In a medium saucepan, add 3 cups of water and salt; bring to a rolling boil. Scrape carrots and cut off the tips and ends. Slice carrots diagonally into 1⁄4 inch pieces (If using baby carrots, just rinse and add to boiling water).

- Add carrots to water and bring to a boil. Reduce heat and continue cooking carrots until tender (approximately 10 minutes).

- Drain carrots and add remaining ingredients. Continue cooking under medium heat until sugar and butter melts and has the consistency of light syrup. Remove from heat. Serves 4.

One medium butternut squash (cut into 1 inch pieces) may be substituted for carrots.

For a little zing, add 1⁄2 teaspoon of orange zest or 1⁄4 cup orange or pineapple juice after carrots are tender.

1 lb. carrots (scraped and cut into 1⁄4 inch slices) or baby carrots

3⁄4 cup sugar (turbinado or white)

1⁄4 cup butter

1 teaspoon nutmeg

1⁄2 teaspoon cinnamon

1 teaspoon vanilla

Dash salt

CRANBERRY SAUCE

1 (12 ounce) bag of fresh cranberries

½ cup water

1 cup turbinado sugar

½ cup orange juice

- Sort and rinse cranberries.

- In a medium saucepan over medium heat, dissolve the sugar in water and orange juice. Add cranberries and stir well.

- Cook mixture until the cranberries start to pop open (about 10 minutes). Remove from heat, stir well and let sit in pan for 10 minutes.

- Pour mixture into a bowl. The sauce will thicken as it cools. Refrigerate until chilled, preferably overnight. Serves 12

FARINA BREAD DRESSING

- Preheat oven to 400°F. In a large mixing bowl finely crumble bread (or use a food processor, it works wonders).

- In a large skillet or saucepan, melt butter and sauté onion, celery, bell pepper and garlic just until tender. Add sage, poultry seasoning and Italian seasoning to sautéed vegetables and stir well. Remove from heat and add vegetable mixture to breadcrumbs and mix well.

- Pour broth over mixture to moisten and stir well. Add the remaining seasonings and stir until well blended. Taste mixture and add additional seasoning if needed. When seasoned to taste, add eggs and blend well.

- Spread the mixture in a large baking/roasting pan (10" x 15") that has been sprayed with a non-stick spray. Bake for 30 to 40 minutes. Serves 10.

2 batches of day old Farina Muffins

1 teaspoon Italian seasoning

1 stick butter

3 to 4 cups broth

2 cups onion, chopped (yellow or white) vegetable or chicken

2 cups celery (finely chopped)

½ teaspoon paprika

1 ½ cups bell pepper (chopped)

½ teaspoon cayenne pepper

3 cloves garlic

½ teaspoon white pepper

1 tablespoon rubbed sage

1 teaspoon sea salt

½ tablespoon poultry seasoning

4 eggs, beaten well

Red or yellow bell pepper may be substituted for green. Or, use all three, It adds color and appeal to the dish.

Diced chicken or turkey may be added to the recipe also (2 cups).

Leftover farina muffins that has been frozen works fine as well. Just remove muffins from freezer 1 day prior to making dressing.

Chef's Tip: Serve with your favorite fish or poultry dish and some homemade cranberry sauce.

Delicious Desserts

CHOCOLATE CHIP COOKIES

- Preheat oven to 350 degrees. Grease 2 baking sheets and place a piece of parchment on each (optional).

- Sift flour, baking powder, baking soda and salt.

- In mixing bowl, cream butter or butter substitute on high speed for two minutes. Add both sugars, honey and mix well (1 minute). Add egg white and vanilla; beat on low speed until well blended.

- Add flour to butter/sugar mixture and mix on low speed. Add chocolate chips until just combined.

- Drop rounded tablespoons of mixture on baking sheets about 2 inches apart or with clean dampened hands, shape into balls first and then place on sheets.

- Bake for 10-12 minutes. Let cookies cool before transferring to wire cooling rack.

1⅓ cups unbleached flour

½ each granulated sugar & firmly packed light brown sugar

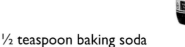

½ cup butter or butter substitute or unsalted butter

1 teaspoon honey

½ teaspoon baking powder

½ teaspoon baking soda

¼ teaspoon salt

2 egg whites

1 teaspoon vanilla extract

8 ozs. semi-sweet chocolate (or dark chocolate) chips

NO-GUILT OATMEAL CRANBERRY COOKIES

½ cup butter or butter substitute (melted)

½ cup raw sugar (granulated can be substituted)

½ cup packed light brown sugar

1 teaspoon vanilla extract

¾ cup unbleached flour

¼ teaspoon each ground cinnamon, nutmeg, and salt

1½ cup old-fashioned oats

¾ cup dried cranberries

In mixing bowl, place melted butter, both sugars and blend well. Add egg whites, vanilla and beat until well blended.

- Sift the flour, baking soda, cinnamon, nutmeg and salt into the egg mixture. Stir in oats and raisins. Refrigerate for 1 hour or overnight.

- Pre-heated oven to 350°, using parchment paper or grease 2 baking sheets. Use a small ice cream scooper or melon baller, scoop cookie dough on to the prepared pans at least 2 inches apart.

- Bake 10-12 minutes until slightly golden. Transfer immediately to wire cooling racks.

- Yields about 32 cookies.

BUTTER COOKIES

- Preheat oven to 350 degrees.

- In a large mixing bowl, with an electric mixer on medium speed, cream butter, sugar, salt and vanilla until light and fluffy (About 15 minutes).

- In a medium bowl, sift flour. Add sifted flour to creamed mixture, one cup at a time, mix thoroughly.

- With a small ice cream scooper, scoop dough and place on ungreased cookie sheet 3 inches apart. Flatten dough with middle three fingers, leaving the imprint. Bake 12 minutes or until cookies are golden brown.

- Cool 5 minutes; remove to wire racks, and cool completely. Makes 18 to 20 cookies.

Chef's Tip: A fork may be used to flatten cookies as well, with prongs of fork, flatten dough by patting lightly. This works just fine.

I pound sweet creamed butter

2 teaspoons vanilla

I cup sugar

4 ¼ cups sifted unbleached flour

Dash of Salt

WHOLE WHEAT GINGERBREAD

½ cup butter

1¾ cups whole wheat flour (sifted)

1 cup brown sugar or honey

¾ cup unbleached flour (sifted)

2 eggs

½ teaspoon salt

1 teaspoon vanilla

2 teaspoons baking soda

1 cup buttermilk

2 teaspoons ginger

1 teaspoon cinnamon

- Preheat oven to 375 degrees.

- Grease and flour 13x9x2 inch baking pan. In a large mixing bowl, with an electric mixer on medium speed, cream butter, sugar and vanilla until fluffy (About 5 minutes).

- Add eggs, one at a time mixing well after each addition. Beat an additional 2 minutes.

- In a separate bowl, after sifting flour, combine all dry ingredients; mix well. Add dry ingredients to creamed mixture alternating with buttermilk, beating well after each addition (about 2 minutes).

- Pour into prepared pan. Bake 30 to 40 minutes or until toothpick inserted in center comes out clean. Cool on cooling rack for 20 minutes. Cut into 3x3 inch squares. Serves 12.

Chef's Tip: Serve plain, with a dollop of whipped cream, or like mama used to serve it – with lemon sauce.

BUTTERNUT SQUASH CAKE

(tastes like carrot cake)

- Preheat oven to 350° F.

- Peel squash carefully and remove seeds. Slice and cook in ¾ cup boiling water until tender. Drain well and squeeze.

- Sift flour, baking soda, baking powder, salt, cinnamon and nutmeg. Set aside.

- In mixing bowl, beat eggs and brown sugar until well combined. Whisk in ½ cup milk and melted butter.

- Add dry ingredients; mix until just combined. Add drained squash; making sure seeds and fibers are removed. Mix in raisins.

- Line a 8 inch baking pan with parchment paper on bottom and oil the sides then flour them. Tap out excess flour then pour in batter.

- Bake until inserted skewer comes out clean; about 45 minutes. Remove from oven and cool completely on baking rack about 15-20 minutes. Invert and peel off parchment paper. Let cool thoroughly.

- To make frosting, combine Neufchatel, butter, confectionery sugar, vanilla, and milk. If too dry drizzle a couple of drops of milk and beat until well combined and smooth.

- Frost top and sides of cake and refrigerate. Remove from refrigerator prior to serving and keep refrigerated between servings.

¾ lb. butternut squash (cooked & drained)

1 cup unbleached flour

¼ cup whole wheat flour

½ teaspoon baking soda

½ teaspoon baking powder

¼ teaspoon salt

1 teaspoon ground cinnamon

½ teaspoon grated nutmeg

1 large egg plus 2 egg whites

1½ cup light brown sugar (firmly packed)

½ cup unsalted butter - room temp. (or butter substitute)

½ cup golden raisins

FROSTING

3 ozs. Neufchatel Cheese or low-fat cream cheese

2 tablespoons butter (or butter substitute)

1½ -2 cups confectionery sugar

½ teaspoon vanilla extract

1 teaspoon milk

OLD FASHIONED HOMEMADE ICE CREAM

12 large eggs (beaten)

1 gallon whole milk

5 cups turbinado sugar

8 cups evaporated milk (5 cans plus ½ cup)

¾ teaspoon salt

6 tablespoons vanilla extract

- Beat eggs well until frothy. In a large pot (preferably a double boiler), mix sugar and salt. Blend in milk gradually, stirring well.

- Cook over medium heat, stirring constantly until mixture begins to thicken, about 12 to 15. Blend in beaten eggs, pouring slowly while stirring. Continue cooking 4 to 5 minutes more, stirring constantly, or until mixture lightly coats a metal spoon. Remove from heat and add evaporated milk. Blend well and let mixture cool down (about 20 minutes).

- Chill custard in the refrigerator, preferably overnight. This is the key to smooth ice cream. Add vanilla to chilled custard and stir well. Freeze in electric or hand cranked freezer following manufacturer's instructions.

- When ice cream is finished churning, transfer to large container, mix well and place in a refrigerator freezer (preferably a deep freezer.

Chef's Suggestion: For a more refreshing taste, use half each of vanilla and lemon extract. For just a little kick, use 4 tablespoons of vanilla and 2 tablespoons of lemon extract. To eliminate cooling time for custard, chill evaporated milk in refrigerator for at least 3 hours prior to cooking custard. Add chilled milk to and extract to mixture, stir well and place in refrigerator. The custard will hold in the refrigerator for up to 3 days.

OLD-FASHIONED CHOCOLATE CAKE

CHOCOLATE CAKE

- Heat oven to 350 degrees. In a small bowl, stir cocoa and boiling water until smooth; set aside.

- Grease and flour two (2) 8 inch round pans.

- To mixing bowl, in large mixing bowl, mix sour cream, sugar and vanilla until light and fluffy.

- Add cup Egg Beaters®, mix well then add remaining Egg Beaters®.

- Combine flour, baking soda and salt. Add alternately with buttermilk to creamed mixture.

- Blend in cocoa mixture. Pour into prepared pans.

- Bake 35 to 40 minutes.

- Test cake before removing. Let cool on cake rack before releasing from pan. Frost as desired.

FROSTING

- Combine butter, cream cheese, vanilla and milk until soft and well blended. Add cocoa powder, confectioner's sugar and salt. Blend until well combined. If too stiff add a few drops of milk and blend. Repeat, if necessary.

BAKING HINT

Since coca powder is acidic, it is usually paired with baking soda, which is alkaline and the two balance each other. While dutch-process cocoa is paired with baking powder as both are neutral. Dutch processed cocoa and regular cocoa are not interchangeable.

CAKE

½ cup cocoa powder

½ cup boiling water (a little less than 1 cup)

2 tablespoon low-fat sour cream

1¾ cup sugar

1 tablespoon vanilla extract

½ cup Egg Beaters®

2¼ cup unbleached flour

1½ tablespoon baking soda

½ tablespoon salt (optional)

1½ cup buttermilk

FROSTING

3 cups confectioner's sugar

½ cup cocoa powder

½ stick butter (room temp.)

3 oz. cream cheese, softened

½ teaspoon vanilla

3 tablespoon milk

Pinch of salt

LEMON POUND CAKE

3 cups unbleached flour

3 cups sugar

Dash salt (⅛ teaspoon)

6 nest eggs

½ cup milk

2 teaspoons pure lemon extract

I teaspoon pure vanilla extract

Preheat oven to 350° degrees. Grease (Pam non-stick spray) and flour 10 inch tube cake pan. Sift flour and salt together in a bowl and set aside.

• Put butter and sugar into a large mixing bowl. With an electric mixer on medium speed, beat ingredients until creamy (10 minutes).

• Add eggs one at a time, beating well after each addition. Continue beating until mixture is light and fluffy (5 minutes).

• Add extract and continue mixing (2 minutes).

• Add flour (one cup at a time) alternating with milk to creamed mixture and mix on low speed until thoroughly blended (2 minutes). Do not over mix.

• Pour batter into prepared cake pan and bake for 1½ hours.

• Let cool in pan on cooling rack for 15 minutes. Invert cake onto cooling rack and cool completely. Glaze or frost (optional). It's delicious plain, glazed or frosted.

Chef's Tip: Try this with the lemon glaze recipe on the next page; it gives this cake a little something extra!!!

LEMON GLAZE

- Mix ingredients well until smooth. If mixture is too thick, add a few drops of lemon juice. If mixture is too thin, add confectioners sugar 1 tablespoon at a time.

- Mix well after each addition until of spreadable consistency. Pour glaze over cake and spread evenly over cake. Gives the pound cake twang!

- Serve with some good old fashioned ice cream. Oops, did I say that?

¾ cup confectioners sugar

3 tablespoons lemon juice (fresh squeezed)

½ teaspoon lemon extract

"NO-BUTTER" BUTTER POUND CAKE

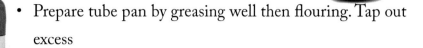

2½ cups unbleached flour

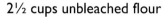

½ cup whole wheat flour

½ teaspoon baking soda

2 large eggs (beaten) or 5 egg whites

(beaten)

½ lb. butter substitute

1¾ cup granulated sugar

1 cup raw sugar

1 teaspoon lemon extract

1 teaspoon vanilla extract

8 ozs. low-fat sour cream

- Prepare tube pan by greasing well then flouring. Tap out excess

- In mixing bowl, put ½ lb butter or butter substitute (room temperature), both sugars and using a paddle attachment, mix on medium speed until very light (about 5-6 minutes).

- Sift together both flours, baking soda and salt set aside.

- To the butter/sugar mixture add the eggs, one at a time and extracts until smooth.

- Reduce mixer speed and ⅓ cup of flour mixture, beat until combined. Add ½ the sour cream, beat until smooth. Add another third of the flour, then, the sour cream. Scrape down sides and beat in last of flour.

- Scrape batter into prepared tube pan bake for 1 hr. 15 minutes or until cake is risen and inserted toothpick comes out clean.

- Cook in pan for about 10 minutes before unmolding onto cooling rack.

HINT

It is best to take room temperature eggs and beat separately before adding to cake batter.

I recommend using parchment paper on bottom of tube pan. It makes removal easier.

To bring eggs quickly to room temperature, place whole uncracked eggs in a bowl of warm water for about 20-30 minutes.

To bring temperature of butter to a proper creaming temperature quickly simply cut into small pieces. This increases surface temperature.

SUGARLESS SPICE POUND CAKE

- Preheat oven to 350 degrees. In a medium bowl, sift flour, cinnamon, nutmeg and salt and set aside.

- Put butter and sucrose in a large mixing bowl. With an electric mixer on medium speed, cream butter and sucrose until smooth (10 minutes).

- Add eggs one at a time creaming well after each addition (5 minutes).

- Add extract and continue mixing (2 minutes).

- Add flour (one cup at a time), alternating with milk to creamed mixture and mix until thoroughly blended (2 minutes). Do not over mix.

- Pour batter into prepared cake pan and bake for 1 1/2 hours. Let cool in pan on cooling rack for 15 minutes. Invert cake onto cooling rack and cool completely. Glaze or frost (optional). It's delicious plain or glazed.

Chef's Tip: The Orange Honey Rum Glaze is marvelous on this cake!

1 lb. butter

½ teaspoon cinnamon

3 cups sucrose

¼ teaspoon nutmeg

6 eggs

½ teaspoon salt

2 teaspoons vanilla

½ cup milk

3 cups unbleached flour

CHOCOLATE ECSTASY CAKE

¾ cup (1 ½ sticks) butter softened

1 teaspoon baking powder

¾ cups sugar (turbinado or white)

1 teaspoon baking soda

2 teaspoons vanilla extract

½ teaspoon salt

2 eggs

1 cup water

2 cups unbleached flour

1 can sweetened condensed milk

½ cup baking cocoa

Milk

- Combine flour, cocoa, baking powder, baking soda and salt in a medium bowl. Stir until well blended. In a large mixing bowl, beat butter and sugar on medium speed until light and fluffy. Add vanilla and mix until creamy. Add eggs one at a time, beating well after each addition. Alternately add flour mixture (1 cup at a time) and water to butter/sugar mixture until well blended.

- Spread into a well greased and floured 13x9 inch pan or two 9-inch round cake pans. Bake in preheated 350° F oven for 25 to 35 minutes or until wooden toothpick inserted in center comes out clean.

- While cake is still hot, use a knife to poke holes (an inch apart) in the top of the cake. Pour the entire can of sweetened condensed milk (1/2 can at a time) over the top of cake and spread evenly with a pastry brush. Allow milk to soak into cake while cake cools. Frost with caramel frosting.

Chef's Suggestion: Serve alone or a la Mode with homemade vanilla ice cream.

CARAMEL FROSTING

- Melt butter in medium saucepan or skillet under medium heat.

- Add sugar and stir constantly until golden brown (approximately 7 minutes). Do not leave unattended, as mixture will burn quickly. Slowly add milk to butter/sugar mixture and continue to stir. The butter/sugar mixture will crystallize once the milk is added.

- Continue to stir until consistency is smooth again (approximately 5 minutes). Reduce heat to low and stir consistently until mixture thickens and is spreadable (approximately 10 minutes).

- Remove from heat and add vanilla. Stir until well blended. Frost cake.

*Note: Unsalted butter may be substituted for salted butter. If substituting, add a dash of salt (1/8 teaspoon) to butter/sugar mixture.

Chef's Suggestion: Use caramel to frost cakes, drizzle over pies or ice cream, or make candy.

½ cup (1 stick) salted butter

1 cup evaporated milk

1 cup sugar (turbinado or white)

1 teaspoon vanilla

HINT

This recipe frosts one 10-inch tube cake; one 15-inch sheet cake or one 8 or 9 inch round two-layer cake.

This chocolate ecstasy cake with caramel frosting is Sis. Kimberly's. You can substitute for butter if you prefer. However, since this is one of her most requested recipes you may want to leave "perfection" alone.

NO FUSS TEA CAKES

½ cup butter (1 stick)

2 cups flour

1 tablespoon vegetable shortening

1½ teaspoons baking powder

1 cup sugar

½ teaspoon nutmeg

2 egg yolks

½ cup milk

1 teaspoon vanilla

2 egg whites

Dash salt

- Preheat oven to 350 degrees.

- Cream butter and shortening until fluffy. Add sugar and cream until smooth (about 7-10 minutes).

- Add egg yolks, one at a time, mixing well after each addition. Add vanilla and cream well. In small mixing bowl, sift dry ingredients. Add to butter mixture, one cup at a time alternating with milk. Mix well after each addition.

- In small mixing bowl, beat egg whites until soft peaks form. Fold egg whites into creamed mixtures just until blended. Do not over mix. Over mixing will make cakes tough. Cover batter with plastic wrap, or transfer to a bowl with an airtight lid. Refrigerate for 1 hour.

- Use a 1 or 2 ounce ice cream scooper to scoop mix and place on greased cookie sheet or drop by a teaspoon onto prepared cookie sheet 2 inches apart.

- Bake 8-10 minutes until lightly browned. Transfer to wire racks to cool. Unused batter can be stored in an airtight container and refrigerated for up to 2 days.

- Store cooked tea cakes in an airtight container. Makes 20-30.

Chef's Tip: For a different taste, use lemon or almond flavor in place of vanilla; and/or use ¼ teaspoon each of cinnamon and nutmeg in place of all nutmeg.

These delicate tea cakes go well with coffee, tea, milk or eaten alone.

BIG MAMA'S BANANA PUDDING

- Preheat oven to 425 degrees. In top of double boiler over medium heat, combine 1 cup sugar, flour and salt. Stir until well blended. Stir in egg yolks and milk. Cook uncovered, over boiling water, stirring constantly until thickened (approximately 12 minutes).

- Reduce heat and cook, stirring occasionally, for 5 minutes. Remove from heat, add vanilla and stir well.

- Spread small amount on the bottom of a 3-quart casserole dish. Cover with layer of vanilla wafers. Top with layer of sliced bananas. Pour 1/3 of custard over bananas. Continue to layer wafers, bananas and custard to make 3 layers of each ending with custard.

- In a large mixing bowl, beat egg whites until stiff but not dry. Gradually add remaining cup of sugar and beat until stiff peaks form. Spoon on top of pudding, spreading to cover the entire surface, sealing the edges.

- Bake 5 to 7 minutes or until delicately browned. Cool slightly and chill, preferably overnight. Serves 16.

If you prefer not to top your pudding with meringue, crush a few vanilla wafers and sprinkle on top of pudding.

1 ½ cup sugar

3 cups milk

½ cup unbleached flour

1 cup whipping cream or ¼ cup corn starch

2 teaspoons vanilla

¼ teaspoon salt

1 box of vanilla wafers

8 nest eggs, separated, at room temp. (yolks only)

6 to 8 medium ripe bananas

Chef's Tip: Use the leftover egg whites to make an angel food cake.

APPLE CRISP

4 cups sliced Granny Smith apples

1 tablespoon minced, crystallized

ginger or fresh ground ginger

TOPPING

⅔ cup rolled oats

⅓ cup packed light brown sugar

¼ cup all-purpose flour

½ teaspoon fresh ground ginger

¼ cup butter, cut into small pieces

- Preheat oven to 400° degrees.

- Arrange apples in a shallow 1½ quart baking dish; sprinkle with crystallized ginger.

- Combine oats, brown sugar, flour and fresh ground ginger in food processor bowl. With motor running, gradually add butter and process until mixture is crumbly. Sprinkle topping mixture evenly over apples.

- Bake in center of oven until topping is lightly browned and crisp, 20 to 25 minutes. Serve alone or with a scoop of vanilla ice cream or a dollop of sour cream. Serves 6.

Hint: Peaches may be substituted for apples. If fresh fruit is not available, canned fruit can be used.

MANGO PEACH COBBLER

- Preheat oven to 375°. Combine all ingredients for filling and mix.

- In a separate bowl, add milk, butter and sugar; stir well. Add remaining ingredients and mix until just combined. Do not over mix.

- In a greased Pyrex baking dish (2.75 quart), pour in filling use a spoon to drop dollops of dough on top. Then using the back of clean spoon, spread dough carefully.

- Back for approximately 20 minutes until dough begins to lightly brown.

- Remove from oven and let cool on rack before serving with whipped cream or vanilla ice cream.

Comments

A'ishah: "Most people are fooled when they taste this as they think its peach cobbler with a tropical twist. Even if you are not a "mango person", you will be pleasantly surprised"

FILLING

2 ripe mangoes (peeled w/ pit removed)

4 ripe medium peaches (peeled and seed removed)

½ cup raw sugar

¼ teaspoon grated nutm

¼ cup apple juice

1 teaspoon corn starch

1 tablespoon lime juice (optional)

COBBLER TOPPING

1 cup unbleached flour (sifted) or ½ cup unbleached & ½ cup whole wheat

½ cup packed light brown sugar

¼ teaspoon salt

¼ teaspoon cinnamon

1½ teaspoon baking powder

½ cup whole milk (2% can be substituted)

3 tablespoon butter (melted)

WINTER SQUASH PIE

FILLING

3 cups cooked winter squash

2 sticks butter (room temp.) or butter or butter substitute can be substituted.

1½ cups sugar

1 tablespoon ground cinnamon

2 tablespoons corn starch

1 12 oz. can evaporated milk

1 teaspoon vanilla extract

3 eggs (or 5 egg whites)

PIE CRUST

1¼ cup flour* plus extra for rolling (unbleached or wheat)

¼ teaspoon salt

1 tablespoon sugar

½ cup butter (or butter or butter substitute

3 tablespoon ice water (plus extra)

*You can use ¾ cup unbleached flour plus ½ cup whole wheat.

FILLING

- Place all ingredients in a mixing bowl and using an electric blender, mix until well blended (about 2 minutes).

- Pour mixture into prepared pie shell. Bake at 400° F for 15 minutes before reducing temperature to 350° for 35 minutes. If edges brown too quickly, cover with strips of aluminum foil.

- Remove from oven and cool on cooling rack until room temperature to set before serving.

PIE CRUST

- In mixing bowl, place flour, sugar and salt in bowl and stir. Cut in butter using a pastry blender or two knives until mixture resembles small peas.

- Add ice water 1 teaspoon at a time and combine until dough comes together roughly. Form into a ball (using only finger tips so as not to add heat from hand) wrap in plastic and refrigerate for at least 30 minutes.

- Remove from plastic, divide in half. Using floured board and rolling pin, shape into a round disk. Repeat with remaining dough for second pie.

CARROT PIE

- Preheat oven to 350 degrees. In a food processor or blender, beat warm carrots until smooth. Add butter, sugar and eggs; mix well. Add remaining ingredients; mix until smooth.

- Pour into deep-dish pie crust shell or bake in buttered 1 1/2 quart casserole or soufflé dish (for soufflé). Bake about 45 minutes or until knife inserted in center comes out clean. Serves 6 to 8.

- Bake about 45 minutes or until knife inserted in center comes out clean. Serves 6 to 8.

Chef's Tip: This pie can be served warm al a-mode with homemade vanilla ice cream; or serve cool, topped with whipped cream. It's so light and tasty. Move over sweet potato pie, you've been replaced!

9-inch unbaked deep-dish pie crust shell

1/2 tablespoon cornstarch

5 medium carrots, peeled, sliced and cooked

½ teaspoon cinnamon

¼ cup butter (½ stick)

1 teaspoon nutmeg

1 ¼ cup sugar (turbinado or white) or ¾ cup honey

¾ cup evaporated milk

1 ½ teaspoon vanilla

3 large nest eggs

Dash salt

KEY LIME PIE

- Preheat oven to 350°F.

- Pour milk into medium size mixing bowl. Add beaten egg yolks and mix well. Pour lime juice into mixture and beat until smooth. Pour into pie crust and bake 15-20 minutes or until center of pie is set.

- Cool completely on a wire rack. Cover and refrigerate at least 3 hours before serving. Serves 6-8.

- *If fresh key limes are not available, Nellie's Key lime juice can be substituted. Also, lemon juice may be substituted for key lime juice, or for a less tart pie; try using 1⁄4 cup each of lemon and lime juice.

Chef's suggestion: Serve with a dollop of whip cream.

1 9-inch graham cracker crust

½ cup key lime juice

1 small can sweetened condensed milk

3 egg yolks (beaten)

FIVE LAYER BANANA SPLIT PIE

2 graham cracker crusts (9-inch)

Whipped cream

CREAM FILLING

1 sticks butter

1 large nest egg

2 teaspoons lemon juice

2 teaspoons vanilla

2 cups confectioners sugar

FRUIT TOPPING

20 oz. can crushed pineapples

4 oz. cream cheese

4-5 large ripe bananas

1-pint fresh strawberries

•

• Drain pineapples. Wash and slice strawberries; removing hull (or stem) set aside. In large mixing bowl, beat butter until creamy. Add sugar, egg, juice and vanilla. Beat until fluffy.

• Pour mixture evenly into both crusts. Arrange over cream filling a layer of each; drained pineapples, bananas and strawberries. In that order. Spread whipped topping over fruit.

• Refrigerate at least 1 hour before serving. Serves 12 to 16. This must be heaven!

Hint: Blueberries or raspberries may be substituted for strawberries.

Breads & Muffins

WHOLE WHEAT BREAD

1½ tablespoons Fleischmann's®
Rapid Rise active dry yeast

1 teaspoon brown sugar

1 cup warm water (105°-115° F)

1½ cup slightly warm buttermilk (90°
F)

¼ cup honey

¼ cup light olive oil

1 tablespoon reduced sodium real
salt

3 cups whole wheat flour

3½ - 4 cups unbleached flour

¼ olive oil

4 tablespoons sage leaves

4 tablespoons rosemary

1 tablespoon basil

1 tablespoon thyme

1 tablespoon salt (can be reduced)

- In bowl, place warm water, brown sugar and yeast. Mix and set aside until foamy.

- In a heavy duty mixer, add 2 cups wheat flour, ¼ cup light olive oil, ¼ cup honey, buttermilk and 1 tablespoon salt. Mix about 1 minute.

- Add 1 cup wheat flour and yeast mixture. Beat about 1 minute. Add remaining flour ½ cup at a time. Change to dough hook as dough gets sticky. Add remaining flour on low speed until smooth and only slightly sticky.

- Using light olive oil, oil a deep bowl and place the dough in. Turn over dough and cover with plastic wrap. Let rise 1½ hours at room temperature.

- After first rise, divide into halves (dough should not spring back up after finger is inserted). On a floured board, roll out 1st half until rectangular. Fold the top third of dough toward center and bottom third up as if making an envelope. Turn sideways and roll dough tightly.

- Press with heel of hand and tuck each end under. Place in loaf pan oiled with olive oil. Sprinkle with half the herbs. Drizzle olive oil lightly over dough. Repeat with other half. Place both loaves away from draft for 1 hour or until double in size. Preheat oven 350° F.

- Place dough in oven and bake for 40-45 minutes. Rotate pans ½ way through baking time. Remove from oven and let sit on cooling rack for no more than 5 minutes.

- Remove bread carefully from baking pans and let rest and cool on racks until completely cool before sealing or wrapping.

- Serve the following day with butter or olive oil.

Hint: Do not allow hot loaves to remain too long in pan or bottom will become soggy.

FARINA MUFFINS

- Whisk together eggs, oil, milk.

- Add cup Farina® or Cream of Wheat®, flours, baking soda, and salt until combined.

- Put into greased muffin pans, fill ⅔ full and bake at 350° for 20-25 minutes.

- Let cool on baking rack before releasing from muffin pan.

- Makes 8.

¼ cup Egg Beaters©

¼ cup light olive or olive oil

½ cup skim milk

½ cup buttermilk

¾ cup Farina© or Cream of Wheat©.

½ cup whole wheat flour

½ cup unbleached flour

½ tablespoon baking soda

I tablespoon sugar

¼ teaspoon salt

FARINA MUFFINS - II

1 cup Farina (Cream of Wheat, Malto Meal)

1 large nest egg

1 cup flour (unbleached/whole wheat or ½ & ½)

1 cup milk

¼ cup sugar (turbinado or white)

¼ cup light olive oil

1 tablespoon baking powder

12 paper muffin cups

1/2 teaspoon salt (optional)

Mazola® non-stick spray

- Preheat oven to 425 degrees.

- Combine all dry ingredients in large mixing bowl. Mix until well blended. In a separate bowl, beat milk and eggs together until mixed.

- Add the light olive oil to the dry Farina mixture and stir just until the dry ingredients are moistened.

- Spoon batter into muffin cups sprayed with Mazola® non-stick and fill 2/3 full. Bake for 15 to 20 minutes, or until golden brown and toothpick inserted in center comes out clean.

- Batter can also be spread evenly in a greased 9x9x2 baking pan; or in a well seasoned 10-inch cast iron skillet.

Hint: For variety, add 1 cup of shredded carrots or cheese, minced onions, bell pepper, corn, jalapeños.

A'ISHAH'S PITAS

In a small bowl, sprinkle yeast and brown sugar over ½ cup of the warm water. Stir to dissolve and let stand until foamy - about 10 minutes.

In mixer, combine remaining water (1 cup), 2 tablespoons olive, salt and 1 cup whole wheat flour. Beat on medium speed until creamy (about 1 minute).

Pour yeast mixture in. Then beat in remaining flour (wheat and unbleached), ½ cup at a time. When dough begins to pull away from bowl sides, switch to dough hook. Knead on low speed - adding 1 tablespoon unbleached flour at a time until dough stops sticking to sides. Beat about 3 minutes. Transfer to greased bowl and turn over to coat.

Cover loosely with plastic and let rise at room temperature until doubled, about 1 -1½ hours. Place a ceramic baking dish in oven upside down and turn over to 400°.

Turn dough onto floured surface and divide into 10 pieces. Form each into a smooth ball and let rest for 15 minutes. Then roll out balls to about 6 inches in diameter. Place each round on floured dish towel and cover until puffy 20 minutes.

Place a cookie sheet in oven for 5 minutes to preheat. Remove and put olive oil on it sparingly. Transfer as many rounds that can fit on cookie sheet and place in oven on top of upside down ceramic dish.

Bake until puffed and light brown (about 7-8 minutes). Stack pitas on plate and cover with clean dish towel. Store after completely cooled in plastic zip bags.

Serve as is or stuff with favorite tossed salad falafel or other fillings.

1½ cups warm water (105° - 110° F)

1 tablespoon Fleischmann's® Rapid Rise active dry yeast

½ teaspoon brown sugar

1½ tablespoon salt

1½ cups whole wheat flour

3 cups unbleached flour

5 tablespoons olive oil

Measurements & Substitutions

3 teaspoons (tsp)	=	1 tablespoon (tbsp)	1 cup	= 1/2 pint
4 tablespoons	=	1/4 cup	2 cups	= 1 pint
5 1/3 tablespoons	=	1/3 cup	4 cups	= 1 quart
8 tablespoons	=	1/2 cup	2 pints	= 1 quart
10 2/3 tablespoons	=	2/3 tablespoons	4 quarts	= 1 gallon
12 tablespoons	=	3/4 cup		
16 tablespoons	=	1 cup		

1 cup granulated sugar	1 cup firmly packed brown sugar or 2 cups confectioners' sugar
1 teaspoon baking powder	1/2 teaspoon cream of tartar + 1/4 teaspoon baking soda
1 tablespoon cornstarch	2 tablespoons unbleached flour
1 cup cake flour	1 cup minus 2 tablespoons unbleached flour
1 tsp fresh grated ginger root	1/4 teaspoon ground ginger
1 tsp nutmeg	1 teaspoon mace
Grated lemon or orange peel	A few drops of lemon or orange extract
Graham cracker crumbs	Equal amounts of vanilla or chocolate wafer crumbs
1 cup plain dry breadcrumbs	3/4 cup cracker crumbs
Romano cheese	Equal amounts of parmesan cheese
1 cup butter	1 cup butter substitute or 2/3 cup vegetable oil
1 cup shortening	3/4 cup vegetable oil
Whole milk	Fat free skim milk or 1% milk
1 cup buttermilk	1 tablespoon lemon juice or vinegar + milk to make 1 cup
1 cup sour cream	1 cup fat free sour cream or 1 cup yogurt or 1 cup fat free buttermilk
1 cup heavy/light cream	1 cup evaporated milk or 2/3 cup skim milk + 1/3 cup vegetable oil
1 oz. (1 sq.) Baking chocolate	3 tablespoons cocoa powder + 1 tablespoon vegetable oil
1 egg	2 egg whites or egg substitute equivalent
Regular bouillon or broth	Low sodium bouillon or broth
1 small clove garlic	1/8 teaspoon garlic powder
Herbs	To substitute fresh herbs for dried herbs, triple the amount of dried herb called for.
2 cups tomato sauce	3/4 cup tomato paste plus 1 cup of water

Notes & Ideas

Made in the USA
Las Vegas, NV
25 October 2021